Returning Light

Resting in the Light

22 Day Teaching Devotional
Amanda Delahoussaye

Resting in the Light

Copyright © 2019
Amanda P Delahoussaye All
Rights Reserved.
ISBN: 9781699856536

Scriptures marked AMP are taken from the AMPLIFIED BIBLE (AMP): Scripture taken from the AMPLIFIED® BIBLE, Copyright © 1954, 1958, 1962, 1964, 1965, 1987 by the Lockman Foundation Used by Permission.

Scriptures marked NIV are taken from the NEW INTERNATIONAL VERSION (NIV): Scripture taken from THE HOLY BIBLE, NEW INTERNATIONAL VERSION ®. Copyright©1973, 1978, 1984, 2011 by Biblica, Inc.™. Used by permission of Zondervan

Scriptures marked NKJV are taken from the NEW KING JAMES VERSION (NKJV): Scripture taken from the NEW KING JAMES VERSION®. Copyright© 1982 by Thomas Nelson, Inc.Used by permission. All rights reserved.

Scripture quotations taken from the New American Standard Bible® (NASB), Copyright © 1960.1962,1963,1968,1971,1972,1973,1975,1977,1995 by The Lockman Foundation Used by permission.

All Greek and Hebrew words are italicized. They are taken from The New Strong's Exhaustive Concordance Of The Bible, James Strong, 1990 copyright© by Thomas Nelson Publishers.

Graphics provided by Pixabay Royalty Free Stock.
Uniquely Mine Editorial Services by Linda A Meaux

CONTENTS

Foreword: 9

INTRODUCTION 11

UNVEILING '7' 15

DEVOTIONAL

Day 1

The Blood 37

Day 2

Love of God 45

Resting in the Light

Returning Light

Day 3

The Seven Spirits of God…………………...51

Day 4

The Fear of the LORD……………………...59

Day 5

Lamp and Light..67

Day 6

Tongues of Fire……………………………75

Day 7

Children of Light…………………………...83

Day 8

All Your Heart……………………………...91

Day 9

Garment of Praise…………………………..99

Day 10

Worship…………………………………….105

Resting in the Light

Day 11

Prayer………………………………...111

Day 12

Thy Kingdom Come……………………117

Day 13

Shadow of Death…………………….125

Day 14

The Fourth Man…………………….…131

Day 15

Entertaining the Light……………….137

Day 16

Godly Sorrow……………………….…143

Day 17

Humility………………………………...151

Day 18

Face of God……………………….……159

Day 19

His Countenance……………………...…167

Day 20

City on a Hill……………………………173

Day 21

Significance……………………………..179

Day 22

Arise! And Shine!...................................185

Resting in the Light

Foreword:

I take pleasure in introducing, fellow Christian author and visionary, Amanda Delahoussaye, whose Godly passion is to help/instruct others in maturing their spiritual growth. You may be familiar with her first book, *Treasure of all Treasures: An Eternal Inheritance.* It endeared readers to her through her humble and gracious style of writing. This book introduced the Plan of Salvation through the use of personal life lessons to bring hungry seekers wanting a more intimate walk with Christ into God's Kingdom.

In her second book, also penned through revelations imparted by the Holy Spirit, "Returning light...Resting in the Light, A 22 Day Devotional" is laid out as a blueprint for understanding how to know God's will and purpose for your journey through life. Each section ends with prayer, a necessary form of daily communing with God.

Amanda guides the reader through self-examination to walk out the principals of what is meant by "Resting in the Light of

Resting in the Light

Christ." Psalm 119:105 "Your word is a lamp to my feet and a light to my path." Darkness vs Light in Gen. 1:-2-3 states, "Darkness was over the face of the deep, and the Spirit of God was hovering over the waters. And God said, "Let there be light; and there was light."

Linda A. Meaux

INTRODUCTION

First, I want to explain the "Why" behind this book. The Lord began dealing with me about my birth order which, I am the seventh of ten children. I began asking, "Why my birth order?" He began to intrigue me with the number seven. It wasn't so much my birth order as it was the number '7' He wanted me to focus on. I am not a numbers person. The Lord doesn't usually speak to me in numbers so, when He began to speak to me about the number '7', I knew He had something significant He wanted to teach me.

In my first book, "Treasure of All Treasures," I talk about the Lord giving me a vision of the Menorah. The Menorah has several different meanings, one being the Light of God or the Light of the Holy Spirit.

Resting in the Light

Returning Light

There is much to learn from the Menorah. I knew immediately there was a correlation between what He was showing me about the number '7' and the vision of the Menorah. In this book, I will discuss the significance of the number '7' to the church in these last days.

Joshua 3:4-5 (GNT)

You have never been here before, so they will show you the way to go. But do not get near the Covenant Box; stay about half a mile behind it. Joshua told the people, "Purify yourselves, because tomorrow the Lord will perform miracles among you."

The main focus of this book as a teaching devotional is intended to give the reader the tools to move into a deeper more intimate relationship with our Lord. It is meant to inspire the reader to search out in more detail where God wants to lead you and what God wants to accomplish through you. It is for the purpose of giving you the insight and principles to apply to your life that will prepare you for the *Returning Light* of

Resting in the Light

God's Glory and equip you to *Rest in the Light*.

This devotional is going to guide you into allowing God to go deeper into your heart. In turn, you will be able to go deeper into the heart of God as it states in Psalm 42:7, deep calls unto deep. We can go only as deep into God as we allow Him to go into us.

My prayer for you is that the Father of Light, the God of our Lord Jesus Christ, would impart to you the riches of the Spirit of wisdom and revelation in the knowledge of Him. That you would know Him through your deepening intimacy with Him.

UNVEILING '7'

In regards to the red fiery heart on the cover, it represents the fiery Light of God's loving heart for His people and what He wants for those who love Him (Song of Solomon 8:6-7). The fiery heart depicts the fire of the love of God being set as a seal upon our heart as with a branding iron. Red depicts the Blood of Jesus which gives us access to the love of God and Light of God's Glory.

Hebrew4christians.com, a Hebrew grammar site states that the number '7' has several meanings. Two meanings being:

1.) *Returning light or Light has returned.*
2.) *Resting in the Light.*

The number seven is one of the most significant number of the Bible because it is the number of spiritual perfection.

Resting in the Light

The number '7' is the most sacred to the Hebrews, to them it represents a perfect World which is crowned in Heaven.

The Holy Bible is the master textbook of all sciences be it physics, chemistry or music. We can see the importance of the number '7' as God has it stamped on all of creation.

I John 1:5

This is the message which we have heard from Him and declare to you, that God is light and in Him is no darkness at all.

Hebrews 12:29

For our God is a consuming fire...

Psalm 104:1-2

O Lord my God, You are very great: you are clothed with honor and majesty, who cover Yourself with light as with a garment, who stretch out the heavens like a curtain.

Resting in the Light

We see from these verses that God is Light or Fiery Light and He is clothed in Light as with a garment. Light in reference to our Creator often refers to God's Glory. The Glory of God is not easy to define. But, when you experience His Glory there is no mistaking it. It is the abundance and splendor of His goodness. At times when He settles His Glory on a person, it feels like the weighty or heavy manifestation of His Presence. Literally it feels like His Glory is pressing down on you.

In the beginning, God created all things to dwell in the Light of His Glory as said in Genesis 1:3. God spoke His Light into the darkness; this was before He created the moon, sun and stars. Light in Genesis 1:3 is defined as *light of life, light of face and Jehovah as Israel's light* in the Hebrew Interlinear.

It wasn't the light from the sun, moon or stars; it was the Light of His Glory that He commanded into the darkness. Adam and Eve were created by Light, for Light, to be clothed in Light and to live in the Light of the Glory of God. This is why they had no shame of their nakedness before God.

They were clothed as with a garment created from the Light of the Glory of God. After the fall, they lost their identity in the Light and no longer lived in the Light but in darkness. As a result, darkness ruled on the earth.

Haggai 2:9

The Glory of this present house will be greater than the Glory of the former house, 'says the LORD Almighty.' And in this place I will grant peace, declares the LORD Almighty.

'Seven' also means *completion,* the end time age or the age of completion, God is going to complete all His promises as this age reaches its completion. With '7' meaning R*eturning Light*, God has returned the Light of His Glory to the church, His house or temple. The latter house will be more glorious than the former house as promised in Haggai 2:9. The Light of the

Glory of God will be intensified and displayed in this hour like never before in history since Adam.

The number '7' also means *maturity*. This is the hour when the sons of God will be manifested in maturity as it says in Romans 8:19. Creation is waiting for the revealing of the sons of God. You and I have the privilege of living in the age where the fullness of the Light of His Glory will be revealed in and through us His sons and daughters. We live in a time when the '7' Spirits of God, which is depicted by the Menorah, will be manifest in the church to display the Light of His Glory and the completeness of His character not seen on earth since before the fall of Adam.

Returning Light

Jesus said in John 8:12 that He is the Light of the world and that if we walk with Him we would have the Light of life. Jesus came to restore and give us access back into the Light of His Glory. Jesus **is** our *returning Light*.

John 12:46

I have come as light into the world, so that everyone who believes in me would not remain in darkness.

The Light of the World came that we would no longer walk in darkness but have our being in the Light of His Glory as intended from the time of creation. We have access to the Father of Light through the Blood of Jesus as stated in Ephesians 2:13. Because we have become complacent and indifferent, the Light of His Glory has not rested upon the church as God intends it to. But, that is changing and it starts with you and me.

Hebrews 4:9-10

There remains, then a Sabbath-rest for the people of God; for anyone who enters God's rest also rests from their works, just as God did from His.

Resting in the Light

Colossians 2:16-17

Therefore do not let anyone judge you by what you eat or drink, or with regard to a religious festival, a New Moon celebration or a Sabbath day. These are a shadow of the things that were to come; the reality, however is found in Christ.

Jesus is our Sabbath. He labored the work of redemption (Passion Week) for six days and on the 7th day or Sabbath He rose again or rested (Luke 23 & 24). We find our salvation in Him knowing it is through faith, by grace and not our works, therefore we rest in Him. Through Christ alone, we rest or settle into a relationship with the Father. This is why remembering the Sabbath and keeping it Holy is in the Commandments. Since His death and resurrection He is our perpetual Sabbath rest (Ephesians2:8).

With Jesus being our Sabbath and returning Light, the Father is returning the Light of His Glory to those who will receive it in this hour. We must seize the moment and walk in Light **now** while it is still light because a time will come when it will be dark and no one can work (John 9:4).

1 Corinthians 3:16

Don't you know that you yourselves are God's temple and that God's Spirit dwells in your midst?

The church, as Blood washed believers in Jesus, is the temple of God which 1 Corinthians 3:16 points out. Jesus who is the Light of the world returned the Light of His Glory to His temple, the Body of Christ.

Luke 4: 16-19

He went to Nazareth, where he had been brought up, and on the Sabbath day he went into the synagogue, as was his custom. He stood up to read, and the scroll of the prophet Isaiah was handed to him. Unrolling it, he found the place where it is written:

The Spirit of the LORD is upon Me, because He has anointed Me to preach the gospel to the poor; He has sent Me to heal the brokenhearted, To proclaim liberty to the

Resting in the Light

captives and recovery of sight to the blind,
To set at liberty those who are oppressed;
To proclaim the acceptable year of the
LORD.

Another word for synagogue is temple. Jesus took His place in the temple on the Sabbath or 7th day as our *Returning Light* to rest or settle in and take dominion just as the Father did at creation on the Sabbath or 7th day. This is a prophetic act stating that Jesus as our *Returning Light* has come to rest upon and in the Church or His Temple. Now, we are called to rest, rule and take dominion in the Light of His Glory with Him in this perpetual Sabbath hour.

The acceptable year of the Lord being defined as the most blessed time when salvation and the free favors of God profusely abound as it states in the Strongs Greek Lexicon. We are living in the acceptable year of the LORD because of Christ our *Returning Light* and our perpetual Sabbath.

Luke 4:18- 19 is describing the anointing upon Jesus which is our inheritance or birthright in the Light. We are permitted to the same anointing to proclaim the acceptable year of the LORD which is our Sabbath in Jesus Christ.

Ephesians 1:11

In Him also we have obtained an inheritance, being predestined according to the purpose of Him who works all things according to the counsel of His will.

Just as Jesus our *Returning Light* took His place in the Temple on the Sabbath to rest or rule in the Light of His Glory, we too must rule and take dominion or rest in the *Returning Light* of His Glory in this Sabbath hour as His Body or Temple. What does that look like? Look at what Jesus did in His ministry. He was anointed to do what is described in Luke 4:18-19, preach the gospel to the poor, heal the brokenhearted, and proclaim liberty to the captives and recovery of sight to the blind, to set at liberty those who are oppressed in the power of His Spirit.

Resting in the Light

The Church will become the mature sons and daughters of Light that all creation groans for in this dispensation, reflecting the likeness of Christ to a dark world. We are to proclaim not only in word but in deed the acceptable year of the LORD while the Lord completes His promises in this hour of completion.

Resting in the Light

Let's discuss the other Hebrew meaning of the number '7', R*esting in the Light.* While rest has a meaning of *inactivity* and *resting from activity in order to relax*, we will be using rest or resting in the sense of the meaning *grounded in; lean into, depend on, place hope in, trust or confidence on or in; to be found in, to settle in, to take residence in or to be located in a specific place or person, to rule in, stop doubt or anxiety.*

Genesis 2:1-3

Thus the heavens and the earth, and all the host of them, were finished. And on the seventh day God ended His work which He had done, and He rested on the seventh day from all His work which He had done. Then God blessed the seventh day and sanctified it, because in it He rested from all His work which God had created and made.

Psalm 121:3-4

He will not allow your foot to be moved; He who keeps you will not slumber. Behold, He who keeps Israel shall neither slumber nor sleep.

We see in Genesis that God created the 7th day for rest which is where its meaning derives from (*Resting in the Light*). Genesis states that God rested from all His work.

God doesn't get tired or exhausted needing rest from activity according to Psalm 121. His strength and power are unfailing; He is all powerful and almighty.

God finished or completed His work of creation, therefore He rested or *settled into* the work of His creation. He took *residence in* His creation to enjoy what He created on the 7th day or Sabbath. Just as the Father rested on the 7th day of His creation,

Resting in the Light

Jesus is resting in this hour, our perpetual Sabbath, in His Body as our Returning Light.

He is causing the Light of His Glory to settle in and take residence in the Church. He is calling us, the Body of Christ, to rest in the Light of His Glory along with Him in this Sabbath hour. He is calling us to learn to *settle in* and *take up residence* in the Light of His Glory. Experiencing His Glory from time to time and *resting in* it are two entirely different things.

Matthew 11:28-30

Come to me, all you who are weary and burdened, and I will give you rest. Take my yoke upon you and learn from me, for I am gentle and humble in heart, and you will find rest for your souls. For my yoke is easy and my burden is light.

With Jesus being our perpetual Sabbath, our calling is to <u>rest</u> in, *lean into, to be grounded in, to be found in or take residence in* the *Returning Light* of His Glory. We are *to depend on, place our hope and confidence in* the Light of His Glory in such a way that anxiety, doubt and fear will find no place in us, which is the *rest* our souls long for. In other words, we must take up *residence in* the Light in order to find *rest* (free from the labor of anxiety, doubt or confusion) for our souls. Jesus is our Sabbath; meaning, He is our rest and all we need is found in Him.

Resting in the Light is peace and much more; Peace through strength, the strength of God's rule. Rest isn't the lack of chaos; it's peace in the midst of chaos. It is taking dominion in and through peace. Trusting in the authority of God to rule and take dominion in the chaos of our lives as well as ruling **through** our lives in the chaos of the world is true rest.

We must *rest* in the Light in order to fulfill our birthright stated in Luke 4:18-19. *Rule* is defined as *exercising authority or dominion*. God the Father *settled in*, *to rule in* and *take dominion in* His creation on the 7th day. Jesus is *settling in* **today**, to *rule* and *take dominion in* His church in this Sabbath hour. As a result, the church will co-labor with

Resting in the Light

Him. *Reigning, ruling, taking dominion*, reflecting the Light of His Glory and proclaiming in word and deed the acceptable year of the Lord on the earth through Him.

Hebrews 4:11

Let us, therefore, make every effort to enter that rest

This verse states that we should labor or be diligent to enter that *rest*. In a baby's life, have you noticed they sleep or rest most of their little lives? That's because while *resting* they do most of their growing. In the same way, as we *rest* in the Light of His Glory, we grow. We become more and more like Jesus. We then become a threat to darkness and the enemy understands this. The enemy will do what he can to hinder our *Resting in the Light*. This is why we must be diligent to enter that rest.

Psalm 8:2-6

Out of the mouth of babes and nursing infants You have ordained strength, because of Your enemies, that You may silence the enemy and the avenger. When I consider

Returning Light

Your heavens, the work of Your fingers, the moon and the stars, which You have ordained, what is man that You are mindful of him, and the son of man that You visit him? For You have made him a little lower than the angels, and You have crowned him with Glory and honor. You have made him to have dominion over the works of Your hands; You have put all things under His feet,

Our Father crowned us with the Light of His Glory at creation. We were created to live, move and have our beings in the Light of His Glory. We lost our birthright of Light at the fall; but, Jesus as our returning Light, has returned it to the Church; it is intensifying in the last days. Ruling and reigning with Christ is what He created us to do; we are created for His Glory. Resting in the Light is exercising the authority Jesus acquired for us through the shedding of His Blood. It is releasing and reflecting the Light of His Glory to eradicate darkness and establish God's kingdom of Light in the world around us.

Resting in the Light

1 Peter 1:19-20

But with the precious blood of Christ, a lamb without blemish or defect. He was chosen before the creation of the world, but was revealed in these last times for your sake.

To fully understand why the Father rested on the 7th day or the Sabbath, we must understand the Father knew from before the creation of the world He was sending His Son who is our *Returning Light* and our perpetual Sabbath. This is why He rested on the Seventh day and not on any other day. Our Creator was *resting* on the Sabbath as a prophetic picture of Him *resting* in the finished work of the cross because, Jesus was crucified from the foundation of the world. Seven has a root word meaning of *oath* and refers to *commitment*. Even then, the Father was making an oath by resting on the 7th day to send His Son to redeem mankind. He could have created all things in a moment but instead He had a strategic plan in all He did.

Jesus, fulfilled His mandate as our *Returning Light. He* came to *rest* in His Temple, the Body of Christ, as our perpetual Sabbath. By this, making an oath, He is committed to building His Church and the gates of hell will not prevail against it. Now, we as the Body of Christ must fulfill our mandate and learn to *Rest* in our *Returning Light* in this perpetual Sabbath hour.

I will never look at the number '7' the same way again. I can see now why the number '7' is special to God because it is rich with revelation of Himself.

In this devotional, I will give you scriptures and insight that will prepare and inspire you to daily search out Jesus our *Returning Light*. The revelation in this devotional will help to equip you to *rest* in the Light of our perpetual Sabbath. Applying the principles in this devotion will put you on the path of the Light of the Glory of God.

God's Light will intensify and shine brighter in this age of completion. He is settling in and occupying His people with the Light of His Glory in this Sabbath hour.

Resting in the Light

We must be prepared. As we learn to *Rest in the Light*, we, the mature (meaning of '7') Sons of God, will fulfill **Luke 4:18-19** - *The Spirit of the LORD is upon Me, because He has anointed Me to preach the gospel to the poor; He has sent Me to heal the brokenhearted, To proclaim liberty to the captives and recovery of sight to the blind, To set at liberty those who are oppressed; To proclaim the acceptable year of the LORD.*

DEVOTIONAL

Resting in the Light

DAY 1
THE BLOOD

Resting in the Light

We said all creation was created in the Light of the Glory of God. We will now talk about the importance of the Blood. The first fact we need to understand is that LIFE is in the blood.

Leviticus 17:11

For the life of the flesh is in the blood, and I have given it to you upon the altar to make atonement for your souls; for it is the blood that makes atonement for the soul.

No one can live without blood flowing in their veins. A team of scientist from Northwestern University have proven at conception when sperm and egg first come together there is a flash of light (we are created from the Father of Lights to be light in the world) and not long after the sperm and egg are joined blood is produced from the sperm.

Before anything else can form there first must be blood because life is in the blood. It is said that science has discovered all matter is congealed light. Even blood is congealed light.

Resting in the Light

Matthew 1:20

But while he thought about these things, behold, an angel of the Lord appeared to him in a dream, saying, "Joseph, son of David, do not be afraid to take to you Mary your wife, for that which is conceived in her is of the Holy Spirit.

Science has discovered it is only after the male sperm has entered the egg that blood can develop. The egg doesn't contain the elements essential for the production of blood. The male element is what produces the blood which produces life. Jesus didn't have an earthly father. Jesus was conceived by the Holy Spirit which means the blood that flowed through His veins was the Life and Light of the Father.

John 1:4

In Him was life, and the life was the light of men.

John 3:5

Jesus answered, "Most assuredly, I say to you, unless one is born of water and the Spirit, he cannot enter the kingdom of God.

Hebrews 9:12

Not with the blood of goats and calves but with His own blood He entered the Most Holy Place once for all, having obtained eternal redemption.

Hebrews 9:14

How much more shall the blood of Christ, who through the eternal Spirit offered Himself without spot to God, cleanse your conscience from dead works to serve the living God.

Just as in the natural, we must have Blood to live spiritually. We attain life and light through the Blood of Jesus to live spiritually which allows us to rest in the Light of His Glory. Leviticus 17:11 states the blood makes atonement for us. To be born again in the Spirit, we need the Blood of Jesus because the Light of Life is in His blood.

Resting in the Light

Jesus with His own Blood has obtained Life more abundantly for us.

The blood of goats and calves in the Old Testament was for a temporary washing of sin and had to be done on a regular basis. The sacrifice of Jesus the Lamb of God was **once** and **for all**. That's the power of His Blood; it cries out for mercy. The Blood of Jesus washes away sin permanently for everlasting life. His Blood gives us access to His Glory; without it we have no access.

Ephesians 2:13

But now in Christ Jesus you who once were far off have been brought near by the blood of Christ.

If you have never surrendered your life to Jesus Christ, let's end this first day's devotional with a prayer of surrender. This is the first step in knowing Him and resting in His Light.

Pray with me:

Father of Light, I thank you for sending Jesus your Son in the flesh as the expression of your love. Jesus, thank you for giving your life and shedding your blood so that I may live.

Forgive me and cleanse me with the blood You shed. Come into my heart and life so I may have access to You, draw near to You and rest in the Light of Your Glory, Amen.

Resting in the Light

DAY 2
LOVE OF GOD

Resting in the Light

Ephesians 3:16-19

*That He would grant you, according to the riches of His Glory, to be strengthened with might through His Spirit in the inner man, that Christ may dwell in your hearts through faith; that you, **being rooted and grounded in love,** may be able to comprehend with all the saints what is the width and length and depth and height—**to know the love of Christ which passes knowledge; that you may be filled with all the fullness of God.***

In order to be grounded (rest) in the Light of the Glory of God, we must first be grounded in His love. We must know, understand and lean on (rest) the love of Christ to be filled with the fullness or the completeness (meaning of '7') of God. An ongoing revelation of the Love of Christ is key to being complete in the Light of the Glory of God; it's essential to resting in the Light.

The words, **to know**, mean *to become acquainted with, to experience and to understand. It is to have intimate knowledge of, to have developed a relationship with*

Resting in the Light

through meeting and spending time with. It is to be sure of something.

Knowing the love of Christ is much more than head knowledge or being able to quote scriptures on the love of God. It's being sure of because of experience and revelation. Intimately knowing the love of Christ because of developing a relationship through meeting and spending time with Him.

In 1 John 4:19, *it states that we love Him because He first loved us.* How can we lean into, trust in, be grounded in and rest in Him without loving Him? How can we love Him without knowing His love for us? To fully rest in the Light of His Glory, we must trust Him. To trust Him, we must love Him. To love Him, we must know His love for us.

Love has many different dimensions as mentioned in Ephesians; it has width, length, depth and height. Many times we have a preconceived idea of what we think love looks like or we define it according to our emotions and standards. If God is love, which He is as stated in 1 John 4, He is the only one who can define love. He is the one we look to in order to know what love looks like; He is our standard of love.

1 John 4:18

There is no fear in love; but perfect love casts out fear, because fear involves torment. But He who fears has not been made perfect in love.

We know according to this verse that love has no fear in it because fear has torment. If fear is tormenting you, you have not been made perfect in the love of God. Knowing the perfect love of God removes fear, doubt and unbelief that keeps us from leaning into, being grounded in and taking up residence in the Light of His Glory. Perfect (meaning of 7) love is complete love; all we can possibly need or desire is found in His love. We are being made complete in His love as we rest or settle in a relationship with Him.

1 John 4:9-10

In this the love of God was made manifest among us, that God sent his only Son into the world, so that we might live through

Him. In this is love, not that we have loved God but that he loved us and sent His Son to be the propitiation for our sins.

This my friend is the ultimate expression of the love of God; He gave His only Son. While we were in our sin not knowing our need of Him. He reached out to us sending Jesus the expression of His love. Revelation says His eyes are like a flame of fire; this is His fiery passionate love for you and me. Ask Him for more experiential revelation of His love and more intimacy with Him.

Pray with me:

**Father I pray that I may start a journey of knowing the width, length, depth, and height of Your love.
Set the fire of Your love as a seal on my heart. In Jesus name, Amen**

DAY 3
The Seven Spirits of God

Resting in the Light

Returning Light

Revelation 4:5

And from the throne proceeded lightnings, thunderings, and voices. Seven lamps of fire were burning before the throne, which are the seven Spirits of God.

In my first book, Treasures of All Treasures, I talk about the vision of the Menorah the Lord gave to me before I knew what a Menorah was. I won't go into great detail about the Menorah in this book as I did in my first book. I will say that I do discuss the different depictions of the Menorah and one is the *Light of the Spirit of God*. Another depiction is the *seven Spirits of God*.

The number '7' is also defined as *fullness*. In relation to the number '7' as far as R*eturning Light* and the Menorah which depicts the seven Spirits of God, God is returning to the Church the Light of the fullness of the seven Spirits of God in this hour. Why? Because time is short; God's desire is that we know Him and we bring those around us into an experiential relationship with Him. It sounds too simple

Resting in the Light

but, it's the truth. We make the mysteries of God's ways to complicated. Too often, we miss or overlook His ways because of the simplicity of them. That's why we must become as little children to enter. He loves to confound the so called "wise."

The Menorah has '7' branches with each branch representing a different characteristic of the Spirit of Light. Isaiah 11:2 lists all the seven Spirits of the Lord. They are:

1. The Spirit of the LORD—Spirit or Breath of God

2. The Spirit of Wisdom—Knowing and applying God's ways

3. The Spirit of Understanding—Supernatural insight into God's ways

4. The Spirit of Counsel—Insight into circumstances and hearts

5. The Spirit of Might—Power and strength

6. The Spirit of Knowledge—Supernatural knowledge not known by natural ways

7. The Spirit of the Fear of the LORD—Reverence and awe for God above all else which will produce submission and surrender to the will of God.

The seven Spirits of the Lord are '7' different expressions or characteristics of the Lord or of the Spirit of Light. Jesus, as a man, walked in the fullness of the Spirit of God meaning He walked in the fullness of all these characteristics of the Spirit of God. If we are to walk as He did, we need to be empowered with the '7' Spirits of the LORD.

Because the Menorah has '7' branches and with the number '7' meaning *fullness or being filled to capacity*, we can say it this way.

The church will walk in the full capacity of the:

1. Fullness of the Spirit of the LORD
2. Fullness of the Spirit of Wisdom

3. Fullness of the Spirit of Understanding
4. Fullness of the Spirit of Counsel
5. Fullness of the Spirit of Might
6. Fullness of the Spirit of Knowledge
7. Fullness of the Spirit of the Fear of the LORD

As the Lord returns the *fullness* of the Light of His Glory to the Church in this hour, we will display the *fullness* of these characteristics of the seven Spirits of God reflecting the likeness of Christ.

Isaiah 55:6

Seek the LORD while He may be found, Call upon Him while He is near.

I believe the Spirit of the LORD is drawing you into a deeper more intimate relationship with Him. He wants to reveal to you the riches of His love and the fullness of His character. Seek the Lord today while He may be found. Seek the fullness of His Spirit

Returning Light

to be able to reflect Christ to the world around you. I declare the '7' Spirits of the LORD in you and upon you in Jesus name.

Pray with me:

I pray Father for the '7' characteristics of Your Spirit to be manifested in my life through Jesus Your Son. Amen

Resting in the Light

DAY 4
The Fear of the LORD

Resting in the Light

First, let's discuss what the fear of the LORD is not.

2 Timothy 1:7

For God has not given us a spirit of fear, but of power and of love and of a sound mind.

It is not a tormenting fear. Tormenting fear is the fear that causes dread and anxiety. The fear that keeps you awake at night robbing you of peace is not the fear of the LORD.

1 John 4:18

There is no fear in love. But perfect love drives out fear, because fear has to do with punishment. The one who fears is not made perfect in love.

We know God is love so there is no fear in God and therefore tormenting fear should have no part in us as a child of God. As we are being made perfect in the love of God, all tormenting fear must go.

Resting in the Light

Proverbs 14:26

In the fear of the LORD there is strong confidence.

The fear of the LORD is what can deliver us from all other tormenting fears that are meant to steal, kill and destroy us. Growing in the fear of the LORD gives us strong confidence in our God. Why? Because, when you understand the majesty and splendor of God and have ongoing revelations of who God is all other fears fade away.

So what is the fear of the LORD?

Isaiah 11:3

His delight is in the fear of the LORD...

> 1. The fear of the LORD is **delightful**.

Psalm 19:9

The fear of the LORD is clean, enduring forever.

> 2. The fear of the LORD is **clean** and it is **forever**.

Psalm 111:10

The fear of the LORD is the beginning of wisdom; A good understanding have all those who do His commandments…

   3. The fear of the LORD is the beginning of **wisdom** and **understanding.**

Isaiah 33:6

Wisdom and knowledge will be the stability of your times, And the strength of salvation; The fear of the LORD is His treasure.

   4. The fear of the LORD is God's **treasure** or **gift** to us.

The fear of the Lord has many facets to it; but, the best way we can define it is as I stated earlier. *Having reverence and awe for God **above all else** which will produce submission and surrender to the will of God.*

As the scripture states, it is a gift from God to His people that holds and releases many different treasures in our lives. Because God is Holy and Just as well as Love, we must

Resting in the Light

possess the fear of the LORD to enter into and sustain a relationship with Him. Without it; His Holiness alone would destroy us. It's because of His love for us that He gifts us with the fear of the LORD **if** we will receive it into our lives.

Acts 5:1-11 is the account of Ananias and Sapphira his wife. God was moving miraculously in Glory and power at that time. These two came before the Lord and lied to the Holy Spirit with no respect and awe for Him. Because of that, the holiness of God struck them dead. It wasn't until the people saw the awesomeness of the holiness of God that they began to walk in the fear of the LORD. Understand, that God doesn't normally go around striking people dead. It is rare but it has happened. He doesn't want anyone to perish. The fear of the LORD keeps us in right standing with Him causing us to understand the consequences of not being in right standing with the Lord.

Psalm 144:3

LORD, what is man, that You take knowledge of him? Or the son of man, that You are mindful of him?

The fear of the LORD produces humility which produces submission and surrender. It give us the correct perspective concerning who God is and where our rightful place is. Who and what are we that the Holy One, the set apart One, the Majestic and exalted One would even consider or be mindful of us? It's only because of His great love for us that He is mindful of us.

Proverbs 19:23

The fear of the LORD leads to life, and he who has it will abide in satisfaction; He will not be visited with evil.

Just as there are negative consequences of not walking in the fear of the LORD, there are positive consequences if we do walk in the fear of the LORD. In Psalm 25:14 the Psalmist says, the LORD confides in those who fear Him. It is our Father's good pleasure to give us the Kingdom which satisfies us with life. The fear of the LORD causes us to be overtaken with the goodness of God. God is good!!

In order to love God, we must understand and walk in the fear of the LORD. You can't have one without the other. Respecting Him for His love only and not the other aspects of His character is not loving or respecting Him fully. We must respect and love Him for who He truly is; not for what we want Him to be.

The fear of the Lord or reverence for God is a response to revelations of who God truly is. So in relation to resting in the Light of His Glory, you can see that the fear of the LORD is the key. Seek Him in His Word and spend time with Him to truly know Him.

Read **Proverbs 2:1-5** to find out how to receive the fear of the LORD. Ask Him to impart the fear of the LORD into your heart by giving you revelation of Himself. Ask Him to help you walk it out in your daily life. And He will give you good treasures in the storehouse of the fear of the LORD.

DAY 5
Lamp and Light

Resting in the Light

Returning Light

Psalm 119:105

Your word is a lamp for my feet and a light for my path.

We discussed since the fall of Adam the world is in spiritual darkness. Let's compare it to natural darkness. Imagine a complete black out after a hurricane, no electricity or lights to be able to find your way around and out of danger. You have a lamp to light your path but you refuse to use it. Not smart! You would remain lost, in danger and groping in the dark. That's what a lot of us do when we refuse to know and follow God's word.

John 1:14 states that Jesus is the Word of God who became flesh. In 2 Samuel 22:29, Samuel is making a declaration that the Lord is his lamp and the Lord will enlighten his darkness. The word of God is a lamp that gives Light to our feet and illuminates the darkness to reveal the path we should walk in. But, it is of no value to us if we don't know it and apply it to our lives. Hosea 4:6 states that His people perish for lack of knowledge. Without the word of God we perish in darkness.

Resting in the Light

Job 12:5

A lamp is despised in the thought of one who is at ease; it is made ready for those whose feet slip.

The word of God is despised by those who think they don't have need of it. It is despised by those who love darkness rather than the Light. It's on hand and ready for the reaching for those who know their need of it in their life. They keep it close and in their heart.

Proverbs 6:23

For the commandment is a lamp, and the law a light; Reproofs of instruction are the way of life.

The commandments and laws of God found in His word are a lamp and light to our path in this dark world. The corrections and instructions of God found in His word bring light and life more abundantly. We flourish with Life in the glow and warmth of God's word just as plants do in the light of the sun.

Colossians 3:16

Let the word of Christ dwell in you richly…

In order for the word to dwell richly in our heart we must read it, search it, and hear it through proper teaching and preaching. We must allow the power of the word to enlighten our understanding to be able to apply it to our life. It's through His word that He gives us wisdom to know His ways and to know the calling that He has called us with as it is stated in Ephesians 1.

Let us not be as those who love darkness rather than light as stated in John chapter 3. Those who love darkness refuse to let the Light of the word of God into their lives. Those who refuse to apply the Light of God's word will remain in darkness.

1 John 1:7

But if we walk in the light as He is in the light, we have fellowship with one another, and the blood of Jesus Christ His Son cleanses us from all sin.

In this verse it is clear that if we walk in the Light of the word of God we have fellowship with Christ. If we have fellowship with Him, we know Him. In Daniel 11:32 it says those who know their God will do exploits. Which means in knowing Him, you will be able to accomplish what you could not do on your own.

How did the prophets of old accomplish the exploits, feats or the impossible? By the word of God and so can you if you walk in the Light of the word of God. These exploits are for those who believe. Psalm 119:130, *The entrance of Your words gives light; It gives understanding to the simple.* In order to rest in the Light of God's Glory we must walk in the light of the Word of God. The Light doesn't follow us, we must follow the Light.

Pray with me:

Father I pray You give me a hunger and thirst for your word. I pray that You give me the resolve to consume Your word

daily to light my path. Illuminate the way in which I should go to fulfill Your plan and purpose for my life. Help me to follow the Light of Your word. In Jesus name, Amen.

Resting in the Light

DAY 6
Tongues of Fire

Resting in the Light

Acts 2:3-4

Then there appeared to them divided tongues, as of fire, and one sat upon each of them. And they were all filled with the Holy Spirit and began to speak with other tongues, as the Spirit gave them utterance.

The disciples here were filled with the Holy Spirit and began to speak in other tongues as the Spirit gave them utterance. This verse says it was tongues as of fire that appeared and sat upon them. The word fire here means fiery Light. They had to be filled with the Spirit of Light in order to speak with tongues which is the love language of God. Tongues of fiery Light is essential for walking in the Light of His Glory. It is necessary in order to walk in the deeper dimensions of God. Fiery tongues fills us with the passion of the heart of God.

Can you be saved and not speak in tongues? Yes! At the time of your salvation the Holy Spirit comes to dwell within your spirit. The baptism of the Holy Spirit is when you walk in a deeper dimension with Him. It's when the Spirit flows as living water to fill you up from within bubbling out of you. We are easily controlled by the Holy Spirit when we allow Him to fill us in baptism speaking with other tongues. It is giving the Holy Spirit the place He deserves in our lives.

Does tongues of fire have to appear when you are filled with the Holy Spirit? No! But, if that is His will for you, tongues of fire will appear. God had a reason for tongues of fire appearing at that time and I believe it had to do with the Holy Spirit coming for the first time in a new way after the resurrection of Christ. He came to dwell within men as opposed to just upon men.

Let me just say here that there is a gift of the Holy Spirit called tongues and interpretation of tongues. This gift not all believers have just as not all have the other nine gifts of the Holy Spirit. They are given out as the Holy Spirit wills.

The disciples in Acts 2 were baptized in the Holy Spirit and at the same time given a gift of the Holy Spirit to speak in languages they didn't know. They were able to communicate the gospel supernaturally in other languages through the Spirit to those around them who spoke other languages. This does and can happen at Baptism but, not always.

We are talking about the tongues of fire and the Baptism in the Holy Spirit where the Holy Spirit gives you a prayer language that is for your edification. It's a prayer language between you and God that enables you to communicate by the Spirit in a more intimate way than if you pray in your understanding.

This prayer language brings you into a deeper dimension in the Spirit of Light. It is a gift that God has given us to keep us filled to overflowing in the Spirit. In Ephesians 5, Paul is urging us to be filled with the Spirit continually and our Holy Spirit prayer language works to do that.

Jude 1:20

But you, beloved, building yourselves up on your most holy faith, praying in the Holy Spirit...

Resting in the Light

We see throughout the book of Acts the disciples were filled continually not just a onetime event. It's an ongoing filling to keep ourselves strengthened in faith. It takes praying daily in the prayer language the Holy Spirit gives you to do that.

Romans 8:26-27

Likewise the Spirit also helps in our weaknesses. For we do not know what we should pray for as we ought, but the Spirit Himself makes intercession for us with groanings which cannot be uttered. Now He who searches the hearts knows what the mind of the Spirit is, because He makes intercession for the saints according to the will of God.

The Spirit of God prays the will of God and the Spirit of God helps our weaknesses. The Holy Spirit knows you better than you know yourself and He knows the heart of God better than we do. It stands to reason that He would pray more accurately the will of God concerning us.

John 16:13-14

"However, when He, the Spirit of truth, has come, He will guide you into all truth; for He will not speak on His own authority, but whatever He hears He will speak; and He will tell you things to come. "He will glorify Me, for He will take of what is Mine and declare it to you."

This verse gives us very important reasons we need the infilling of the Holy Spirit on a daily basis. The Holy Spirit not only builds up our faith and helps our weakness but He stirs up the gifts He has placed within us. He shines the Light on truth to guide us into all truth. He knows the secrets of the heart of God and tells them to us. He will glorify Jesus so we can see Him clearly and glorify Jesus to the world around us.

If you have been baptized in the Holy Spirit with evidence of tongues, pray in tongues daily for at least 15 minutes a day. We must be born again to receive the baptism in the Holy Spirit. If you haven't been filled with the Holy Spirit and speak with other

Resting in the Light

tongues, I urge you to pray and ask Jesus today to give you tongues of fiery Light.

Luke 11:9 says, *"Ask, and it will be given to you."*

Pray with me:

Jesus, I thank you that you have saved me and now I ask that You baptize me in the Holy Spirit and enable me to speak with fiery tongues, Amen. Now by faith begin to speak in your unknown tongue.

Returning Light

DAY 7
Children of the Light

Resting in the Light

Returning Light

As I said earlier, you were made in the Light of the Glory of God. In 2016, scientist captured images of the flash of light that sparks at the moment of conception when the sperm meets the egg. At that moment, billions of zinc atoms explode releasing a brilliant light signifying the eggs viability to survive. There is a flash of light starting the conception of every human being.

Genesis 1:3

Let there be light

When God said let there be light, it was His expression of creative activity by which at conception you became light in Christ. You were made by the Light, for the Light and for the purpose of *Resting in the Light*. The first Adam lost our spiritual inheritance of Light and the second Adam, Jesus, restored it to us.

Ephesians 5:8-9

For you were once darkness, but now you are light in the Lord. Walk as children of the Light. (for the fruit of the Spirit is in all goodness, righteousness and truth)

Resting in the Light

What does it mean to walk as children of the Light? First of all, we need to understand what light does in the natural. It illuminates, it reveals, it gives energy, and it dispels darkness. As it is in the natural so it is in the spiritual, meaning everything in the natural can teach us something spiritually.

The number one thing we should understand as children of the Light is that the Light within us dispels darkness in us and around us. As a child of the Light when you walk into a room where there is dark activity, that darkness is more afraid of you than you are if it. The darkness wants to flee seven different ways to get away from the Light that is in you. You should have no fear of darkness if you are truly a child of the Light.

When you walk into the presence of people who are walking in darkness, the Light in you will illuminate or bring to light their dark ways sometimes without you saying a word. This is why they may feel uncomfortable around you. Light and darkness cannot have fellowship together. It makes them uncomfortable unless they repent.

The Light you walk in will illuminate truth and reveal Jesus to the world around you. It will give energy which is vitality, momentum and strength not only to you but those around you. The closer you get to the Light the more you see and the clearer you see.

To walk is to *conduct one's life and live in a certain manner*. Walking in the Light is walking in the manner Jesus walks. I John 4:17 states as Jesus is, so are we in this world. It is conducting our lives in such a manner that it reflects the Light of Life or reflects Jesus to the world around us. It's reflecting the attributes of His character.

To walk as Jesus walks, we must know Him and His ways. We do that through His Word, spending time with Him in prayer and aligning our lives with His will. Jesus said when you have seen Me you have seen the Father because He was reflecting the Glory of the Father. In that same way, we should reflect the Glory of the Son. This will be a

Resting in the Light

---

reality in the church more than ever. As we submit to Him, God will fulfill and bring His promises to completion ('7') in this age of completion.

The miraculous will become more common place than ever before as we walk in the Light and as the Light of His Glory intensifies. The day of the LORD will be a reality in our lives and people will be drawn to the Light of His Glory in us.

Scientist have come to realize that we are made up of Light thus confirming the creation account in Genesis when God created all things in the Light of His Glory. We were created to walk as children of Light. Choose this day whom you will serve and choose to walk in the Light as Christ is in the Light. If you are in Christ, it's who you are, not who you are trying to be. Search the scriptures for yourself as it states in John 5:39; they testify of who Jesus is.
Walk in the Light as Jesus is in the Light.

Pray with me:

Father in Jesus name, I pray that you would give me revelation of my identity as a child of the Light. Jesus help me to know You that I may walk in the Light as You are in the Light. Amen

Resting in the Light

DAY 8
All Your Heart

Resting in the Light

Returning Light

Jeremiah 29:13-14

And you will seek Me and find Me, when you search for Me with all your heart. I will be found by you, says the LORD, and I will bring you back from your captivity…

The Amplified Bibles says it this way:

Then (with a deep longing) you will seek Me and require Me (as a vital necessity) and (you will) find Me when you search for Me with all your heart. I will be found by you, 'says the LORD,'

  Have you ever wondered why God doesn't just show Himself to everyone in such a way that there is no question of His existence? Like, God should just part the clouds and make Himself known to everyone? Romans 1:28 says that man in his rebellion does not like to retain God in their knowledge so God gives them over to their own way. If we don't care to know Him, He leaves us to our own way until and if we do want to know Him.

Resting in the Light

  Jeremiah says God does want to be found by those who seek Him with a deep longing for Him. Those who seek Him as though He is vitally necessary. Found by those who truly want to know Him and His ways versus those who don't really want to know Him.

  There is a purpose in the seeking. God is a person who desires a relationship with us. He longs for you to desire Him. He will not and does not want to force Himself on anyone. For example, if you want to marry someone, you want that person to want to marry you. You don't want that person to be forced to marry you. Where is the joy in that? He wants you to want Him.

  God wants to be loved and pursued by you. The pursuit itself produces longing and yearning. It produces anticipation and excitement. When we search for Him with all our heart, we have the promise that we will find Him. The words "find Me" in verse 13 is defined as *to be lighted upon, to appear, to cause to light upon, and to cause to encounter.* In finding Him or encountering Him, He enlightens us with the Light of His Glory. He shines on us with the Light of His Glory to reveal Himself or to appear.

There may be times we don't feel like seeking but, we don't live by our feelings. We live by the Word of God. When we seek Him in spite of our feelings and out of pure obedience, we will find Him.

Psalm 97:11

NIV—Light shines on the righteous and joy on the upright in heart.

There is Joy in seeking the LORD. Have you ever seen a child at an Easter egg hunt? The excitement, enthusiasm and joy they express when they are looking for an egg is contagious. And they want to hunt again and again. Matthew 18:3 says,
"Unless we become as little children, we will never enter the kingdom of heaven."
How much more excitement and enthusiasm should we have in our search for the One who created us.

Resting in the Light

Matthew 13:44

Again, the kingdom of heaven is like treasure hidden in a field, which a man found and hid; and for joy over it he goes and sells all that he has and buys that field.

What a Treasure GOD is! This man in Matthew sought this Treasure at all cost holding nothing back. As we seek God with our whole heart at all cost, the Light that God shines on us produces joy unspeakable and full of Glory both in the searching and finding. Seeking builds anticipation and appreciation for the Treasure.

Verse 14 of Jeremiah 29 says, as we seek Him we will find Him and then He will bring us out of captivity. The children of Israel found themselves in a desperate place because they turned away from God. God told Jeremiah to tell the children of Israel if they would seek Him again with all their heart He would be found by them. In seeking and finding Him, we find not only joy but freedom from our captivity. We find freedom from the sin that keeps us bound in slavery.

Isaiah 55:6

Seek the LORD while He may be found, Call upon Him while He is near.

I believe God is near to you today or you wouldn't be reading this book. Are you one that truly wants to know Him and His ways? I want to encourage you today to seek the LORD while He may be found. Don't hide yourself from the LORD. Practice daily spending time with Him in prayer, His Word, and among His people. You won't regret it.

Resting in the Light

DAY 9
Garment of Praise

Resting in the Light

Returning Light

Read Isaiah 61:1-2

Isaiah 61:3

And provide for those who grieve in Zion—to bestow on them a crown of beauty instead of ashes, the oil of joy instead of mourning, and a garment of praise instead of a spirit of despair. They will be called oaks of righteousness, a planting of the Lord for the display of His splendor.

In verse 1 of Isaiah 61, it states that the Spirit of the Lord is going to accomplish all these things in verses 1 through 3 in the year of the Lord's favor which is **Now**. Verse 3 talks about the garment of praise. In Psalms 104:2 it states that the Lord covers Himself with Light (Light of His Glory) as a garment. This is the same garment talked about in Isaiah 61:3. It is a garment of the Light of His Glory that God wraps around us as a garment when we praise Him. The more we praise Him the brighter the garment gets.

As we make praise a part of our relationship with God and as that garment of Light gets brighter, we then become firmly planted in the Lord. This means we can't be persuaded out of our relationship with Him. A display of His splendor we become to the world around us. The word splendor here means *the magnificent characteristics and qualities of.* We will display or reflect the magnificent character and qualities of God the Father of Lights like the different facets of a diamond. We will experience beauty instead of ashes (fragmented debris due to war) and the oil of joy instead of mourning.

Psalm 100:4

Enter into His gates with thanksgiving, and into His courts with praise. Be thankful to Him, and bless His name.

Thanksgiving and praise are closely related. We cannot draw near to God without thanksgiving and praise. Thanksgiving acknowledges God's goodness even when our circumstances are not good. It acknowledges all the good things God does for us. Giving thanks is necessary to entering into His gates. Gates are the points of entrance into the Presence of God. We are to verbally give thanks, yes.

But, it is more important to have a heart or attitude of thanksgiving then it will automatically flow out of us. Out of the mouth the heart speaks (Luke 6:45).

Praise acknowledges God's greatness and majesty. It acknowledges who God is. Praise ushers us into the courts of God which relates to intimacy with Him. Praise escorts us deeper into the Presence of God.

Psalm 22:3

But you are holy, Enthroned in the praises of Israel.

The word enthroned means *to make a throne for ruler ship, to cause to dwell, to sit and remain.* Our praise creates a throne for God to come and take His rightful place in our heart as King to dwell and rule in our lives.

Being thankful and expressing thanks takes intentional practice. We must train ourselves to be thankful and to intentionally express it to God. The same goes for praise. To train yourself, read out loud sections of the book of Psalms to God in your prayer times.

I pray as you begin your journey of praise that your garment of Light would increase in radiance and shine as the Son.

DAY 10
Worship

Resting in the Light

Psalm 96:9

Worship the LORD in the splendor of His holiness. Tremble before Him, all the earth.

Worship is a response to the holiness of God. Worship acknowledges the holiness of God. When you get a revelation of the holiness of God you can't help but tremble in worship before Him. Holiness means *one who is set apart, like no other, and sacred.* Worship is a response to a revelation of the sacredness and total uniqueness of God knowing there is no other like Him.

John 4:23-24

"But the hour is coming, and now is, when the true worshipers will worship the Father in spirit and truth; for the Father is seeking such to worship Him. "God is Spirit, and those who worship Him must worship in spirit and truth."

To truly worship in spirit and truth, we must be in relationship with Jesus. In the Gospel of John Jesus says He is the Way, the Truth and the Life. The only "Way" to

"Truly" worship the Father is through Jesus. The word spirit refers to the deepest part of your being which powers your feelings, thoughts and actions. True worship involves our feelings, thoughts and actions. Worshiping in spirit and truth is worshiping in all sincerity through Jesus with your whole being.

Genesis 22:5

He said to his servants, "Stay here with the donkey while I and the boy go over there, We will worship and then we will come back to you."

Surrender and obedience is true worship. Genesis chapter 22 tells of the account when God told Abraham to sacrifice Isaac his son on the altar. Isaac, meant more to Abraham than his own life. Abraham was willing to surrender his all (Isaac) to God in order to obey God. God never intended Abraham to harm Isaac but was testing Abraham's loyalty. God stopped Abraham before Isaac was harmed because God Himself gave the sacrifice of His Son from the foundation of the world (Revelation 13:8). The highest form of worship is obedience to God. True worship is holding nothing back from Him and in turn He gives us all He is. We get the better end of the deal.

Worship is about an experience not just theology or religion. It is all about God's worth and worthiness. We enter His gates with thanksgiving, His courts with praise until His presence is manifest. His experiential presence will produce true worship and this will produce surrender and obedience.

Although, worship does entail singing, dancing and different forms of outward expressions, it is more the way we live and our lifestyle. Outward expressions of worship are good and is part of worship. But, if we are not obedient to God, it is only lip service which is hypocrisy. The Lord sees the heart.

Daily, set your heart to enter His gates with thanksgiving and His courts with praise until you experience His revealed Presence. Worship Him in the beauty of holiness which will produce surrender and obedience in your life. This, my friend, is resting in the Light.

Pray with me:

Father in Jesus name make me a true worshiper, one that worships You in Spirit and Truth. Amen

DAY 11
Prayer

Resting in the Light

There are many forms of prayer but, the one form of prayer I will focus on is the prayer of the "pursuit of God." Prayer as the pursuit of God involves humility and it says, "God I need you, I'm nothing without You, I must know you and your ways. I want to experience You."

There is a difference between ritual prayer and prayer as a dialogue between you and the Creator. It's talking to God but, more than that, it is listening to God. It isn't giving God marching orders; it's getting marching orders from God. Time set aside each day to pursue God conditions our heart for true communion with God. We must consider prayer or communion with God as a privilege not a duty.

Communion is defined as *sharing or exchanging of intimate thoughts and feelings.* Yes, God wants to share His thoughts and feelings with you. He has feelings and emotions. This is why we have them, because we are made in His image and His likeness. He wants to share His thoughts and feelings with you as well as you sharing yours with Him. The pursuit of God is wanting to hear the voice of God more than wanting to be heard.

I Thessalonians 5:17

Pray without ceasing.

Prayer is a heart condition. It directs your heart continuously to God. Not just as a once in a while ritual but as a continuous pursuit of God in all things.

Throughout Jesus's life on earth, He demonstrated His need for communion with His Father. If Jesus needed to pursue His Father, how much more do we?

I will give a short outline of the prayer of pursuit given in the tabernacle of Moses as depicted in the book of Exodus. For more detail read my book *Treasure of All Treasures*.

1. Outer Court – Washing with the Blood of Jesus. It is through the Blood of Jesus we have access into

His Presence. Come into prayer asking for the cleansing of the Blood of Jesus

2. Inner Court or the Holy Place – Welcome the Holy Spirit to come fill and direct you. Ask the Holy Spirit to reveal Jesus to you. Begin to give God thanks leading into praise and wear praise as the garment of Light that it is.

3. Holy of Holies -- You will experience the Light of His Glorious manifest Presence which is the goodness of His Presence. Worship Him in the beauty of Holiness.

Matthew 7:7

Ask, and it will be given to you; seek, and you will find; knock, and it will be opened to you.

Seek means *to crave, to strive after and to aim for.* To knock here means *to knock with a heavy blow.* In other words, pray with unwavering fervent determination to find and discover God.

Jeremiah 29:12-14

Then you will call upon Me and go and pray to Me, and I will listen to you. And you will seek Me and find Me, when you search for Me with all your heart. I will be found by you, says the LORD...

Have you ever looked back at your life and realized that God was there at a time you didn't realize He was there? Or, have you looked back and realized God was pursuing you before you started to pursue Him? That's what I call God's peek-a-boo moments. Is He playing a sick game? No, not at all. He gives us hints that He is present and wants to be found by us. There is so much more He wants to share with you and so much more you are in need of. Pursue Him and you will find Him.

I pray that we all recognize God's peek-a-boo moments in our lives.

DAY 12
Thy Kingdom Come

Resting in the Light

Returning Light

Matthew 6:10

Your kingdom come. Your will be done on earth as it is in heaven.

One purpose Adam had before the fall was to establish the Kingdom and will of God here on earth as it is in heaven. With the fall, He lost that privilege. Jesus, the second Adam, restored that privilege back to us with His Blood. This is our mandate and inheritance.

Before we can affect the world around us with the Light of the Glory of God, we must first allow God to establish His Kingdom and His will within us. We can't expect to implement God's Kingdom and will in the Earth if it isn't first established in us. If we live our own way and resemble the kingdom of darkness, we don't have the authority or power to establish God's Kingdom and His will on the earth.

What does it mean to establish God's Kingdom and will in us? In the Gospel of Luke Jesus says that the Kingdom of God is within you. If we are in Christ, the Kingdom of God is within us; where the King is there is His Kingdom. Because the Holy Spirit resides within, we have the ability to live according to the Kingdom of God and the will of God. He will not force it upon us; we must choose to live it. He puts life and death before us but we have to choose one or the other.

Romans 14:17

For the kingdom of God is not eating and drinking, but righteousness and peace and joy in the Holy Spirit.

God's righteousness, peace and joy is the Kingdom of God. We must allow the Holy Spirit to establish these characteristics in our own life before we can implement them in the world around us. Notice, we can't have peace or joy without first allowing God's righteousness to be established. Don't be mistaken by thinking you have to have all your ducks in a row for God to use you. Remember the Blood of Jesus imputes God's righteousness to us. We are all in the process of allowing God to develop His Kingdom within, which is sanctification. As long as we are allowing the process, God will use us. God's grace is sufficient.

The Blood of Jesus imputes righteousness to us and then, we must learn to walk it out in our lives. It's a process; there is purpose in the process. The purpose is to form Christ in us. Righteousness is defined as *the condition acceptable to God, the way in which man may attain a state approved of God, integrity, virtue, purity of life, rightness, correctness of thinking, feeling and acting.*

God's will must be established in order for righteousness to be established. Then you will have peace and joy that follows. This is done only by the power of the Holy Spirit within us. It must be about God's Kingdom and will, not ours. Our way leads to death; God's way leads to righteousness, peace and joy in the Holy Spirit. If you are looking for peace and joy, allow God to establish His Kingdom and will in you. Those around you will be influenced by that same peace and joy in you.

Resting in the Light

Galatians 5:22-25

But the fruit of the Spirit is love, joy, peace, longsuffering, kindness, goodness, faithfulness, gentleness, self-control. Against such there is not law. And those who are Christ's have crucified the flesh with its passions and desires. If we live in the Spirit, let us also walk in the Spirit.

Galatians describes the kingdom of God and how to establish it in our lives in order to establish it in earth. The fruit of the Spirit must be cultivated or developed in our lives by the power of the Spirit. It takes training to crucify our will and passions to live God's will and passions. It's choosing life or God's way and not our own which leads to death. Be patient with yourself; God is.

Pray with me:

Father, you are high and lifted up and there is no one like you. I pray that You by the power of Your Spirit establish Your kingdom and will in me. Father, work Your will in me to do Your good

pleasure in all things until my greatest joy is to do Your will. Father, help me to apply Your kingdom in the earth as it is in heaven. Amen

Resting in the Light

DAY 13
Shadow of Death

Resting in the Light

Returning Light

Psalm 23:4

Yea, though I walk through the valley of the shadow of death, I will fear no evil; For You are with me; Your rod and Your staff, they comfort me.

Resting in the Light of the Glory of God doesn't suggest we will not have trouble, tribulation or trials in this life. On the contrary, in the Gospel of John, Jesus tells us we will have tribulation in this world but to be of good cheer because He has overcome the world. Rest isn't the absence of conflict; rest is peace in the conflict.

In some of these seasons of difficulty, we may <u>feel</u> like we are in or we may actually be in a valley of death. In these dark times of trial and tribulation, Jesus said in Hebrews that He will never leave us or forsake us. His rod and staff refers to His *comfort* and *support* in our times of dark trials.

In Psalm 23 it states that we walk **through** the valley of the shadow of death. When we look for Him in the valley and allow Him to comfort and support us in our distress, He will always walk us through and out to victory. It's a process. There is purpose in the process; that purpose is the development of the fruit of the Spirit within us. In other words, it's for the purpose of forming Christ, the Light, in us. We are not meant to stay in the valley; this too shall pass. Those in Christ have victory even in death because it leads to eternal life with Christ.

2 Corinthians 12:9

And He said to me. "My grace is sufficient for you, for My strength is made perfect in weakness." Therefore most gladly I will rather boast in my infirmities, that the power of Christ may rest upon me.

Grace here refers to *God's joy, pleasure, delight, good will, loving-kindness and strength* which He bestows upon us in our times of weakness and trials if we receive it. His grace is sufficient meaning it is *unfailing*, *strong enough to defend* while He walks us through our deep dark seasons. His grace *satisfies* us and makes us *contented* in our times of weakness or frailty if we receive it.

Returning Light

Isaiah 45:3

I will give you the treasures of darkness and hidden riches of secret places. That you may know that I, the LORD, who call you by your name Am the God of Israel.

The Light of the Glory of God strengthens and enables us to shine brightest in the dark seasons of life. He will give you weapons in the dark places to make you victorious over the dark. His Light is a weapon over the darkness. He will supply you with all you need to overcome in your valley of the shadow of death. He will shine His Light on treasures and hidden riches you can find only in the dark and secret places of the valleys.

As He leads you out of the dark season, you will be armed and dangerous to the enemy of your soul. You and those around you will know that He is LORD and it is by His hand you are victorious. Trust Him in the pain and through the process.

Pray with me:

Father, I thank you for your rod and staff that comfort me in my dark seasons. I thank you for Your grace that is sufficient for me in my weakness. Help me to see Your Light which is Jesus in my dark hour. Father, shine Your Light in the dark season to reveal Your treasures and hidden riches, in Jesus name, Amen.

DAY 14
The Fourth Man

Resting in the Light

Returning Light

Daniel 3:25

"Look!" he answered, "I see four men loose, walking in the midst of the fire; and they are not hurt, and the form of the fourth is like the Son of God."

Shadrach, Meshach, and Abednego were bound and thrown into a fiery furnace that was turned up seven times hotter than usual. They were facing death because they refused to worship any other God but the true God. The men who were given the order to bind them up and throw them into the fire were killed by the heat when just approaching the furnace.

After the three Hebrew men were thrown in the furnace, the King looked into the furnace and saw four men in the fire instead of three. He said the three men were not bound any longer and walking around in the fire not harmed. The fourth man looked to be the Son of God. In the midst of a literal fiery trial these men were bravely facing, the fiery Light of the Glory of God over powered and overshadowed the fire that was meant to kill them. God's fiery Light unshackled the

Resting in the Light

Hebrew men from what was binding them and they were found rejoicing with Jesus in the midst of the fire within the fire.

Hebrews 13:5

For He Himself has said, "I will never leave you nor forsake you."

Jesus is there in your fiery trial with the fiery Light of His Glory. He knows about the trial you will face before you face it. He is in the trial before you face it ready to show Himself faithful to you. The Light of the Glory of God doesn't keep us from fiery trials it protects us **in** them and unshackles us from what binds us while walking through the trial. It's the holy fire within the fire. He has a purpose for the process; trust Him in it.

Isaiah 49:25

I will contend with those who contend with you, and your children I will save.

Just as God opposed the men who had bound and thrown Shadrach, Meshach, and Abednego in the fiery furnace, He will contend with the enemy on your behalf. What the enemy means for your harm God will turn it around for your good. The enemy is no match for the One who created him.

Revelation 2:10

Be faithful until death, and I will give you the crown of life.

The three Hebrew men saw such a marvelous deliverance because they remained faithful and true to God even in the face of death. Look for Jesus and His Light in the trial to guide you through the process. Draw on the strength of God when you are going through fiery trials. We will have trials in this life regardless if we are in Christ or not; I'd rather go through them with Christ than without Him. Don't waste the trials of this life; allow God to refine you and set you free in them.

Pray with me:

Father, I ask that You help me to see Jesus, the Light of Your Glory, in the trials I go through. Strengthen me to

remain faithful to You in the trials and deliver me from the things that bind me. Help me to trust you in the process, in Jesus name. Amen

DAY 15
Entertaining the Light

Resting in the Light

John 14:21

He who has My commandments and keeps them, it is he who loves Me. And he who loves Me will be loved by My Father, and I will love him and manifest Myself to him.

God's benefits and promises are conditional. If we love God, we will obey Him and align our lives with His will (John 14:15). God loves everyone but, when we obey Him, we are enjoyed by Him and given favor by Him. Obeying God brings with it the promise of God manifesting Himself to the one who obeys. Manifest is defined as *to display or show, to appear or demonstrate, to prove oneself.*

Obedience to God is entertaining or making oneself enjoyable to God. As a result, you are making Him welcome and attracting His Presence to you in such a way that He will display and demonstrate the Light of His Presence in your life. He will prove Himself or show Himself faithful to those who love and obey Him.

Resting in the Light

Isaiah 1:19

If you are willing and obedient, you shall eat the good of the land.

If we are willing and obedient, it creates an atmosphere that attracts the Light of His Glory. It creates an atmosphere that God enjoys and feels welcome in. As a result, even the goodness the land has to offer, which is its beauty and prosperity, you will enjoy.

Exodus 19:5

Now if you obey me fully and keep my covenant, then out of all nations you will be my treasured possession. Although the whole earth is mine

Even though all the earth is the Lord's and the fullness thereof, to be treasured by God is our goal. In obeying God, we become His special treasure. One that He not only enjoys being with but, one He watches over, guards and protects with close attention. We want to be one that He treasures above all else.

Returning Light

We attract His Light in our willingness and obedience. We rest, settle in and take up residence in the Light by our obedience. We can't settle for just willingness; we must be willing and obedient. Determine in your heart today to align yourself with the will of God for your life. We must live a life that creates an atmosphere that is conducive for the Glory of His Presence to dwell. As you walk out His will in your life, which is a process, the Light will get brighter and watch God manifest Himself and prove Himself to you.

Pray with Me:

Father in Jesus name, I ask you to show me where I need to be obedient to Your will. I pray You give me the will and the ability to do Your good pleasure in all things until my greatest joy is to do Your will. Amen

Resting in the Light

DAY 16
Godly Sorrow

Resting in the Light

Repentance is defined as *godly sorrow, a turning away from sin and turning to God, aligning yourself with the will and ways of God, a change of mind.* Godly sorrow is *being made to feel remorse over sin that leads to salvation and a change of direction.* It is not guilt and condemnation that will plague us and keep us in bondage.

Initial repentance is when we receive Christ into our heart and life. To be born again, there must be repentance from darkness into Light and from unbelief to belief in Christ and the work of the cross. If you haven't yet surrendered your life to Christ, please go to Day 1 to read and pray the prayer of salvation.

I want to focus on repentance as a way of life for the believer in Christ. A way of life for the one who wants to R*est* in the R*eturning Light* of the Glory of God and to keep our fellowship with the Light as it states in 1 John 1:7.

What do I mean by living a life of repentance? Look at sin as if it is a dam that blocks a refreshing flow of water. Sin blocks the flow of the Spirit in our lives. It stops the flow of freedom, peace, joy, love, power and Light. We all fall short; as the Light of God shines on us and in us, we will see in ourselves ways that are not God's way or character.

This is what light does; it reveals both God to us and sin in us. As we see these areas of sin in our lives, it should generate godly sorrow that leads us to turn from those ungodly ways and change our direction to God's ways. Repentance is giving God the space that sin use to occupy in our life. Each time we repent of sin, we give Jesus the Light more space in our lives and the Light in us gets brighter.

What is it that justifies or gives us right standing with God? The fact that we turn away from a particular sin or the Blood of Jesus? The Blood of Jesus is what justifies us. Turning away from sin without justification is just a change in life style. In true repentance there will be a turning away from sin and turning to Jesus Christ trusting in His work of redemption.

Returning Light

Repentance breaks the dam that blocks the flow of the Spirit of God which brings a refreshing in our life. Our Father didn't send His Son to suffer and die the humiliating death He died so we would live our life the way the devil wants us to live (Hebrews 10:29). No, He did so that we would be able to live our life as a reflection of Jesus. Grace is the power of God that enables us to live as the Father wills. But, as stated in 1 John 2:1 if we do sin, we have an advocate Christ Jesus. His mercy is new every morning and His Blood remains sufficient and always will be sufficient to cleanse us from all sin we repent of. This is grace!

2 Corinthians 7:10

For godly sorrow produces repentance leading to salvation…

None of us are perfect. There is only one perfect and He is God. In the process of becoming like Jesus, we will fall. Our humanness should not be an excuse to sin or to remain in sin; it should propel us into seeking the Light of the World (Jesus) trusting in the power and grace of God that can change us. Godly sorrow produces in us the desire to be quick to repent in order to stay in fellowship with the Light.

Matthew 3:8

Therefore bear fruits worthy of repentance

This verse is telling us to give evidence of repentance. In other words if we truly repent, our actions will reflect it. Our actions and life style if godly will be proof of repentance. If someone is murdering, stealing, cussing etc., you know that person isn't in right standing with God. In the same way, if a person is loving Jesus, loving people and implementing acts of kindness you can say that person is showing fruits of repentance.

Why is repentance so important?

Matthew 4:17

From that time Jesus began to preach and to say, "Repent, for the kingdom of heaven is at hand."

Here the kingdom of heaven is referring to *a territory subject to the rule of the King or the reign of the Messiah. It refers to the royal power, dominion and rule of the King.* Repentance gives the kingdom of heaven, Jesus the Messiah and King, the authorization or permission to reign, rule and have dominion in your territory or your life.

Acts 3:19-20

Repent therefore and be converted, that your sins may be blotted out, so that times of refreshing may come from the presence of the Lord, and that He may send Jesus Christ, who was preached to you before

The presence of God moves in as a result of our repentance. Times of refreshing in His presence comes as a result of repentance. These times of refreshing and reviving in His presence are absolutely vital to our spiritual survival. It is a prelude to *Resting in the Light*. Repentance is an invitation for Jesus Himself who is the Light of Life to invade our life and space. It is an

Resting in the Light

invitation for the activity of heaven to be among and in our lives.

Please take a minute, allow the Light of God to shine and show you areas in your life that need to be repented of so His presence can bring refreshing and revitalize your soul.

DAY 17
Humility

Resting in the Light

Psalm 138:6

Though the Lord is on high, yet He regards the lowly; But the proud He knows from afar.

I want to start off by saying what pride does. Pride causes God to resist us (James 4:6). It causes God to be far from us because He hates pride. Pride is what caused Satan to fall from an angelic worshiper of God to the devil we know of today. If we are harboring anger, offense, and bitterness, we are in pride. Pride is the root of these things. Forgive and let it go!

Micah 6:8

He has shown you, O man, what is good; And what does the LORD require of you but to do justly, to love mercy, and to walk humbly with your God?

What is walking humbly with God? And, why is it necessary? Humility draws us into intimacy with God and intimacy with God produces humility. Humility draws the Light of the Glory of God to you.

Resting in the Light

Numbers 12:3
(Now the man Moses was very humble, more than all men who were on the face of the earth)

What was it that made Moses more humble with God than all other men at that time?

Numbers 12:7

Not so with My servant Moses; He is faithful in all My house.

In this verse it says that Moses was faithful to God. Moses obeyed God because Moses trusted God. Obedience to God is trusting God and that is humility. You can't trust and obey God without humility. Humility says, "God I trust You and I obey you because You know better than me. I am nothing without You." To trust and obey God, we must know His Word. His Word is His will revealed.

Humility is knowing your need of Him and knowing your place compared to Him. It is thinking of God's will and desire above your own. Wanting His will and way more than your own. Honoring and giving the Glory due to the LORD while not seeking our own honor or Glory is true humility.

Because of humility, God talked with Moses face to face as stated in Numbers 12:8. Humility draws the face of God towards you. Moses had such intimacy with God that God avenged him when Aaron and Miriam spoke against Moses. How would you like God to appear to you and rebuke you because you were talking against someone close to Him? Not me! I want to be the one God takes up for. God talked to other prophets in dreams and visions as in a dim glass meaning not plainly. Not with Moses, He talked plainly to Moses and told Moses His secrets face to face.

Isaiah 57:15

For thus says the High and Lofty One who inhabits eternity, whose name is Holy: "I dwell in the high and holy place, with him who has a contrite and humble spirit, to revive the spirit of the humble, and to revive the heart of the contrite ones.

This is where God dwells, with the humble and contrite, with those who know their God and with those who know He is High, Lofty and Holy. If we want to dwell and rest in the Light of His Glory, we must walk humbly with Him.

There is One greater than Moses and that's Jesus Christ. Humility is the character of Christ. Jesus walked in humility with His Father. He did only what the Father instructed Him to do as stated in John 5:19. If Jesus walked in humility with the Father, how much more should we.

1 Peter 5:5-6

Likewise you younger people, submit yourselves to your elders. Yes, all of you be submissive to one another, and be clothed with humility, for God resists the proud, but gives grace to the humble. Therefore humble yourselves under the mighty hand of God, that He may exalt you in due time.

Humility isn't beating yourself up or degrading oneself. Humility is submitting to God and one another. It is preferring others over yourself. Looking out for the interest of others is true humility. Exalting ourselves over others is pride, the opposite of humility. Humility doesn't exalt oneself over others; it exalts us over sin, circumstances and the enemy.

Humility is the mark of maturity. It's walking in obedience and trust in the difficult times as well as the good. It's rejoicing in what God has done for us, not in what we do for Him. It's by His grace alone that we can do anything.

Pray with me:

Father in Jesus name, I ask that You forgive me for the lack of humility in my life. I pray that you develop in me the character of Christ that I may walk in humility before You. Amen

Read Philippians 2: 3-15

Resting in the Light

DAY 18
Face of God

Resting in the Light

Returning Light

Numbers 6:25

The LORD make His face shine upon you, and be gracious to you

Shine is defined as *a quality of brightness from reflected light.* The face of the LORD is Light which reflects a quality of brightness, not known to man. We want the face of God to shine upon us with the Light of His Glory.

Psalm 27:8

When You said, "Seek My face." My heart said to You, "Your face, LORD, I will seek."

Why would the LORD instruct us to seek His face?

The face of the LORD depicts several attributes of God. The eyes depict God seeing you.

1. He sees where you are physically, spiritually and emotionally. He knows the meditations of our hearts and the thoughts of our mind. He

sees our struggle and our weakness as well as our strengths. There is nothing hid from Him. He wants to give us His vision that we would see with His eyes.

Revelation 1:14

His head and hair were white like wool, and His eyes were like a flame of fire.

This is my favorite attribute of His eyes. It depicts a fiery passionate love for you and me. It is the fire of the love of the Bridegroom in the Song of Solomon. A jealous and zealous love that is pure and intense for you and me.

    2. When the face of God shines on us, we experience the revelation of His love.

1 Peter 3:12

But the face of the LORD is against those who do evil.

When someone turns their face from you, it is a sign of broken fellowship. In

Deuteronomy 31:17 and 18, the Lord is talking about hiding His face from His people because they went after other gods and did evil in His sight. As a result, there is no protection for the people when God turns His face from them.

   3. It stands to reason that when God's face shines upon us there is protection.

Being face to face with someone depicts fellowship and intimacy. It's getting to know the thoughts and heart of someone.

Numbers 12:8

I speak with him face to face, even plainly, and not in dark sayings; and he sees the form of the LORD.

   4. His face shining upon us depicts intimacy. God reveals His secrets and His ways as He shines His face on us. He wants intimacy with us.

Resting in the Light

1 Peter 3:12

For the eyes of the LORD are on the righteous, and His ears are open to their prayers...

The ears of God depict God leaning His ear into your direction because He is eager to hear your voice. You have the ear of the LORD. He listens to you and hears what is on your heart. When you call on Jesus, He will answer you (Jeremiahs 33:3).

Job 33:4

The Spirit of God has made me, and the breath of the Almighty gives me life.

Song of Solomon 1:2

Let Him kiss me with the kisses of his mouth- for your love is more delightful than wine.

5. Out of the mouth of God will come the breath of God which is His Spirit. He comes to breathe life into us and our circumstances. He removes deadness from us and gives life more abundantly. His mouth depicts

delightful intimacy with Him. He will whisper to His beloved (you and me) His secrets. He will smile upon us which depicts His favor.

Numbers 6:25

...And be gracious to you.

Gracious is defined as *kindness, goodness and generosity*

6. God's face shining upon you reveals His goodness and graciousness.

2 Corinthians 3:18

But we all, with unveiled face, beholding as in a mirror the Glory of the Lord, are being transformed into the same image from Glory to Glory, just as by the Spirit of the Lord.

7. Just like a mirror reflects the sunlight, when He shines His face upon us, we become His reflection, reflecting the Light of His Glory.

Resting in the Light

The LORD is calling you to seek His face. As you do, you will develop a delightful intimacy with Him. I pray the LORD make His face to shine upon you in Jesus name. Amen

DAY 19
His Countenance

Resting in the Light

Returning Light

Numbers 6:26

The LORD lift up His countenance upon you, and give you peace.

You notice a person's countenance by the demeanor of their physical body. When someone is sad, depressed, anxious, happy, peaceful, excited, angry etc., you can usually see it on their countenance. The countenance of a person is the outward expression of what is going on inside of them.

God's countenance is the outward shining of all His goodness, love, peace, joy etc. going on inside of Him. His countenance is the expression of His nature. God does grieve over sin. But, because Jesus is our remedy for sin, His countenance never changes (Hebrews 13:8).

James 1:17

Every good and perfect gift is from above, coming down from the Father of the heavenly lights, who does not change like shifting shadows.

Resting in the Light

God is never depressed, sad, anxious, worried, or insecure. He is always joyful, peaceful, happy and courageous. Our circumstances may be scary and overwhelming to us, but not so to God. His perspective is much different from ours until we take on the countenance of God.

His countenance must flow from our inner man which flows outward to be seen by others. We can receive or reject it. It begins with receiving Jesus Christ as LORD of our lives. We can't have the Light of His countenance shining on the outside unless we first have the Light of Christ on the inside.

The countenance of God lifts us up from discouragement to the courage of God. It lifts us up for others to see and be drawn to the Light of the countenance of God upon us. Our countenance is like a mirror of what is going on inside of us.

The more intimacy we have with God the brighter the Light of His countenance shines through us. It's simple, but not easy; this is why we need the Holy Spirit. Jesus said the Holy Spirit will lead us into all truth.

The LORD in this hour is wanting to shine His countenance upon us to be the expression of His nature to the world around us. He wants all His goodness to be in us flowing out of our countenance to be seen by men in order to draw men to Himself.

1 Peter 3:15

But in your hearts revere Christ as LORD. Always be prepared to give an answer to everyone who asks you to give the reason for the hope that you have. But do this with gentleness and respect

As your relationship with Christ grows more and more intimate, the Light of the countenance of God will shine in and upon you for your good and for the good of those around you. Be ready to explain to people what it is they see in you. Be ready to explain what Jesus has done for you and why they see such hope and Light in your life. Do this in gentleness and respect.

Pray with me:

Father in Jesus name I ask for more intimacy with you. I ask for the Light of Your countenance to be in me and to shine through me. Help me to be able to explain to others what it is they see in me and upon me. Amen

DAY 20
City On A Hill

Resting in the Light

Returning Light

Matthew 5:14-16

You are the light of the world. A city that is set on a hill cannot be hidden. Nor do they light a lamp and put it under a basket, but on a lampstand, and it gives light to all who are in the house. Let your light so shine before men, that they may see your good works and glorify your Father in heaven.

In Christ, we are the Light of the World. Light in its nature is luminous and meant to be seen. Have you ever turned on a lightbulb and didn't see light (unless it's burnt out) or didn't see light from the sun? It is impossible not to see light. So it is with the people of God. If we are resting in the Light, it will be seen by those around us.

You will hear people say things like: I love being around you because you are so up lifting, you are so encouraging, you have such joy and peace or you are a witness of Christ's love. That is the Light of His Glory shining in and through you.

When flying in an airplane at night, if the sky is clear, it is a beautiful sight to see a

Resting in the Light

city lit up with bright and beaming lights. In the same way, it is a beautiful sight to our Father to see His people shining brightly together with the Light of His Glory.

Imagine being lost in a dry, dark desert surrounded by nothing as far as the eye can see. You are hoping to see a glimpse of a flicker of light to guide you in the darkness. Suddenly, you see light from a city in the distance. Seeing just a glimmer of light gives you hope in the darkness. In the same way when you shine with the Light of God's Glory, it gives hope and life to those in darkness around you.

Matthew 5:16

Let your light so shine before men, that they may see your good works and glorify your Father in heaven.

This is what the world is yearning for. They are waiting for Light and hope in their darkness. Jesus wasn't put under a bushel to be hidden from the world. He was the Light of the World and He shined brightly. He didn't hide in secret places or dark corners.

Returning Light

He lived to shine brightly for all to see the Glory of the Father. We as His children are to do the same.

Luke 11:35-36

See to it, then, that the light within you is not darkness. Therefore, if your whole body is full of light, and no part of it dark, it will be just as full of light as when a lamp shines its light on you.

If the Light of Life dwells within us, it is impossible not to see. Unless, our light is darkened; sin will dim or darken our light.

1 John 2:15-16

Do not love the world or anything in the world. If anyone loves the world, love for the Father is not in them. For everything in the world—the lust of the flesh, the lust of the eyes, and the pride of life—comes not from the Father but from the world.

We are not to shy away from the world. We are to be in the world to love and influence the world with the Light of the Glory of God. But, if we are influenced by sin and its

Resting in the Light

darkness, our light will be darkened and dim. Repentance and the Blood of Jesus is the remedy for dim and darkened Light.

1 John 2:1

My dear children, I write this to you so that you will not sin. But if anybody does sin, we have an advocate with the Father—Jesus Christ, the Righteous One.

If you find your Light has been darkened by sin, turn away from that sin and allow Jesus to cleanse you with His Blood. Shine! Like a city on a hill as you are intended to!

Pray with me:

**Father, I have sinned (Confess particular sin). Forgive me and wash me with the Blood of Jesus. I pray
that the Light in me would Shine brightly in the world around me as a city on a hill in Jesus name, Amen.**

DAY 21
Significance

Resting in the Light

The definition of significance is *worth, value, importance and identity.*

John 6:9

There is a lad here who has five barley loaves and two small fish, but what are they among so many?

Jesus was in the wilderness with 5000 hungry people. Testing His disciples, He asked His disciples about feeding them. The disciples were perplexed and in bewilderment not knowing how they were going to feed so many people on a mountain in the wilderness. He told his disciples to feed them.

Jesus knew exactly how He was going to feed them. He knew there was a young boy who seemed to be insignificant to all those around him. This young boy held an insufficient amount of food. In the hands of Jesus, this insignificant child became significant and was used in the purpose of God for the Glory of God. Suddenly, the small amount of food he had became more than sufficient to feed 5000 people with left overs.

If you are feeling insignificant with nothing or little to give, take courage and hope. If the truth be told, we are all insignificant with nothing to give outside of Christ. The young boy and his food would have perished in the wilderness along with the 5000 if it were not for Jesus. In Christ, we find our significance. In Christ, our nothing or little becomes more than enough.

Satan is very good at taking half-truth and deceiving us. He knows without Christ, the Light of the World, we are insignificant and no match for him. But, he also knows that in Christ we are significant and we have authority and power over him.

The CEO of a very successful fast food restaurant found his significance in Christ. All he had was a piece of chicken on a bun. But, in the hands of Jesus, that chicken on a bun became more than enough. That restaurant is Chick-fil-A. The founder of Hobby Lobby found his significance in Jesus as well. All He had was a paint brush and a can of glue. In the hands of Jesus, that became more than enough.

Luke 10:38-42

...And Jesus answered and said to her, "Martha, Martha, you are worried and troubled about many things. But one thing is needed, and Mary had chosen that good part, which will not be taken away from her."

Mary, Martha's sister, found her significance in Christ at His feet, resting in the Light of His Glory. Martha, although well meaning, tried to discourage her and accused Mary of wasting time. Martha was looking to other things for her significance, as a result she was troubled with worry and anxiety.

Jesus lovingly corrected Martha to let her know what Mary was doing was the one very significant thing we must all be doing. That is to be found in Christ resting at His feet in the Light of His Glory through the Word, prayer and seeking His face. Don't get me wrong, faith without works is dead faith, but we don't find our significance in our works, any other thing or person. We find our significance in Christ alone; as a result, we walk out our faith by our works.

I pray that you rest at the feet of Jesus and find your significance in the Light of His Glory. Consequently, Jesus can use your life to feed many around you as He did with the young lad.

DAY 22
Arise! And Shine!

Resting in the Light

Returning Light

Romans 13: 12 - 14

The night is far spent, the day is at hand. Therefore let us cast off the works of darkness, and let us put on the armor of light. Let us walk properly, as in the day, not in revelry and drunkenness, not in lewdness and lust, not in strife and envy. But put on the Lord Jesus Christ, and make no provision for the flesh, to fulfill its lusts.

Armor of light is the Light of the Glory of God used as our armor of protection and warfare. The Lord is inviting us to put on the Light of His Glory or to put on Christ who is the Light of the World.

Just as when light is shined in your eyes, because of its brilliance, you can't see anything in or past the light. In the same way, the enemy is blinded by the Light of the Glory of God. He cannot see us if we are Resting in the Light. This is what it means to be hidden in Christ. Step into the Light and allow Him to become your shield, guard, and armor.

Resting in the Light

Isaiah 60:1-4

Arise, Shine; For your light has come! And the Glory of the LORD is risen upon you, For behold, the darkness shall cover the earth, and deep darkness the people; But the LORD will arise over you, and His Glory will be seen upon you. The gentiles shall come to your light, and kings to the brightness of your rising. Lift up your eyes all around, and see; they all gather together, they come to you; Your sons shall come from afar, and your daughters shall be nursed at your side.

Let's look at the first word in verse one, *Arise*. It means to *make a stand in a firm fixed position, to come on the scene, and to confirm.*

With this definition in mind, we can see that we have a role to carry out in order to shine with the Light of His Glory. We must make a *firm and fixed stand* to make our Light *known* in order to *confirm* the Light of His Glory to the world around us. In other words, how will they know unless we *Arise* and let His Light S*hine* through us? How will they know unless we reflect Christ to those around us?

For those of us in Christ Jesus, your Light has come! Jesus has given you access into the Light of His Glory; it is risen upon you. What we must do is *Arise*! Come on the scene in a fixed and firm position, and walk in His Light in such a way that we confirm to the world around us that He is here and alive.

Deep darkness covers the earth and the people in it. And God has made a way in Jesus for all to come into the Light. They must see the Light in us as we *Arise* and S*hine* with His Glory. People will be drawn to the Light within us. Where they see no hope, they will see the Light of Hope emanating from within us.

In Isaiah 60:7, it says that the Lord promises to glorify the house of His Glory. The word glorify in this verse is defined as *to beautify, to adorn with beauty*. The word house in this verse is defined as *a dwelling place, a habitation*. If we are in Christ, we are His habitation; He dwells within us. We are the house of His dwelling Light, which means as we make a firm stand to shine with the Light of His Glory, the Lord's Glory beautifies us and makes us attractive to those around us seeking hope. Those in desperate need of hope and salvation will be drawn to the Light they see within us.

We are living in the last days when God is increasing the Light of His Glory. And the latter Glory of this house will be greater than the former.

If you apply these principles to your life in walking with the Lord, you will be on the path of the Light of the Glory of God. The only hope for our loved ones, for our sons and daughters is if you and I choose to "*Arise!* And S*hine!*" with the Light of His Glory. And they too will see and know Him.

Pray with me:

Father, I pray that You would give me a resolution in my heart to <u>Arise</u> to make a *firm* and *fixed* stand to <u>Shine</u> with the

Returning Light

Light of Your Glory in this hour. That those around me will see and know that they may have the same hope of Glory in Christ Jesus. Amen!

Resting in the Light

Made in the USA
Columbia, SC
22 March 2021